also by lisa panepinto

on this borrowed bike

where i come from the fish have souls

nature of infinity
lisa panepinto

SPUYTEN DUYVIL

New York City

ISBN 978-1-963908-97-8
cover photo by the author

Library of Congress Control Number: 2025946708

CONTENTS

wanderer

wild friend

tributaries

my kayak engulfed
in silver cloud
ocean fog so thick
i couldn't see

gray seals appeared
circled my boat
swam between me
and rock island
keeping me from capsizing
in icy currents

dog faced swimmers
supernatural eyes
of the deep

children of ocean
leading me
safely to shore

on blue rushing river

ancient body
lined with cedar
pines and maple

saying a wish
for happiness
and no suffering
for anyone
made of her
star water

coyote and owl
being themselves
singing wildly

leaping salmon
cleansing the channels

cormorants riding
the eddies my kin

singing *rock me*
on the water

taking bottles out
of waves
returning butterflies

floating under bridges
atop a boat

hawks shining
from beach wood shore
the guiding light

sweet fern scent
washing the stones
making all new

from the depths
of unseen spring
coming to a holy place

lake mother welcoming me
just as i am

glistening source
of shelter lifeblood
for thousands of beings

ice shifting sounding
like whale song
her heartbeat

forest jewel

haloed in fur
pregnant-looking
bobcat rested
under sugar maple
looking at me
with emerald eyes
black gold
camouflaged face

i wanted to stay
mesmerized by its beauty
but turned away
to avoid scaring

sensitive one
nurturing the embryo

the entire universe
being reborn
above my head

bright floating heart
always with me
life of my life
giving breath to me

fields of wild roses
pollen-covered bees
the light always
carrying me

i give myself to
i belong to

bird choirs recreating
the day with devotion

a prayer for mercy
and goodwill
throughout all spheres

eye of the hill opening
sparkling paths of jade

sawing chaga

holding onto birch
swaying with grandmother

snow flurries spread white silk

i lit a candle
and heard wingbeats

giant blue raven athlete
floated over tree line

i said *hi* from bright birch

*

talking to the sun
she listens

*

by her glance let me
return to the source
to know i am
always hers

eyes closed
i felt quick innocent airy feet
touch my palm
totally alive
golden nuthatch
ate seed from my hand

*

my hands planting marigold
seeds in the night
tiny black and tan
bodies able to fly and sprout
lush flowers
from whispered prayers

on a pilgrimage to blue springs

silent meditator
loud flyer
grouse with me

movements sounding amplified
in mythic cloud forest
wild nests all around

rock tripe and star-tipped
lichen hills
of wandering roots

anointing with myrrh
as *catch the wind* played
i laughed
a prayer
to the great mother

seeing screech owl
enshrined in ancient tree
my success and equanimity

sublime meditative
shining in sun
eyes halfmoons
mirroring everyone

i felt i would see
owl before i saw her
shades of light
expansive beatitude of clouds
power of flight

not wanting to take

pictures of divinest scenes
hawks perched on icy oaks

women holding umbrellas
walking children to school

crosswalk guards smiling
guiding the fledglings

miracle of rivers merging into one
consecrating the land

baptized

on john baptiste day

in hillside waves

with floating lilies

looking back to shore

a panther with amber eyes

swam out to me

we ran the beach smiling

aspen leaves rustling

before the castles were built

and pontoon boats came

i was disintegrated
then returned
to the land

my medicine came
from yarrow alchemy

tamarack boughs
covered in goldleaf

monarch emerging
from cocoon portal
orange bright
radiant new
brilliantly patterned
resting after metamorphosizing

silent as sun
not even needing acknowledgment
of miracle feat

born for the beauty of transformation
clinging to blue asters

newborn at the bmv

now serving 180 at window three
said the loudspeaker

i waited with ticket 204
masked in farthest corner

a mother held her infant
son named atticus
a few seats down

a teenage girl waiting
for her license said
cute baby smiling

she commented on all
who walked through the bureau
i wish i had his robe
way to park
she's out there with a bong
i should ask for some

atticus' uncle said
he'd die without weed

the teen recalled her drunk mother
talking to the wall

her mother repeated
i don't want grandkids

the newborn baby
sheathed in light
purified the place
with primal wisdom

you submerged yourself in the lake
then reappeared
with three lit candles

one in each hand
and one balanced on your head

walking on water
wearing a crystalline robe

carrying the fire
no waves can wet

emerging from
the lake returning to the lake

waterfalls cascading
on blue stones

deer jaw
smiling in sun
dropped in snow
by coyotes

spruce roots
walking uphill

white skull and antlers
feeding lichen
guardian streams
nourishing a thousand
new deer

raccoon

looking at me   nearly invisible from behind a mask
holding the bark of ponderosa pine
hands freshly cleaned by the creek
melded with the shine

holding the bark of ponderosa pine
gone inward where others can't see
melded with the shine
witnessing the universal body

gone inward where others can't see
the outer world reflects my devotion
witnessing the universal body
raccoon on granite cliffs by the ocean

the outer world reflects my devotion
a wave of consciousness
raccoon on granite cliffs by the ocean
absorbed in the source of kindness

a wave of consciousness
appearing in the middle of the road
absorbed in the source of kindness
raccoon tells me love is all there is to hold

appearing in the middle of the road
beyond this masked persona
raccoon tells me love is all there is to hold
what i once thought friend is poison

beyond this masked persona
intuitive knowing guides me through the wilderness
what i once thought friend is poison
raccoon's at home in darkness

intuitive knowing guides me through the wilderness
kin with everything the water cloaks
raccoon's at home in darkness
invisible behind a mask

litany

singing on bear mountain
as protective amulet

a pure hearted child
loon called out

dolphins carry underwater light therapy
and healing algae

cleansing polluted shores with songs
removing fishing lines from netted whales

passing high frequency clicks
through coral reefs with meditative breath

naming each other in syllabic tones
dolphins rest in sand shelter coves

journeying beyond the clank of oil rigs
war submarines and wire debris

dolphins swim with one eye open and alert
one eye closed and dreaming a new start

after hurricane maria

i stood in line at home depot
                    what i want to know

is what's happening in puerto rico
                            the cashier said to his coworker

do they have lights
                he received no answer

as he rang up my supplies
                        a us territory left to shake without aid

thousands still living in tents
                    do they have lights

the cashier repeated
                gazing down aisles

as if his strong wish could restore damaged homes
                                        plant trees

give lights
        to all in need

in mourning for black worshippers
murdered at church
during bible study
by a young white supremacist

i keep drumming to aretha
wishing for sweet water
to mend the hearts of traitors
who kill their own savior

marching across indigo cliffs as vigil

for neighbors shot

in bowling alley nightclub

synagogue and church

remembering mother's words
don't harm anyone
i'm inside all

a blessing for bobcat
and fox to stay
untrapped and unsighted

the embodiment of kindness
was shot over theft of electric guitar

the smiling angelic one was murdered
on the freeway a victim of road rage

who was trying
to get home to her mother

wildcat with emerald eyes
singing jon batiste *let god lead*
wildcat who remains
unseen but retains the power
of the universe wildcat
who intercepts bullets
and can't be killed or burned
wildcat who protects the vulnerable
miracle nurse pharmacy earth
wildcat who holds impenetrable
immaculate love like the sun

blue jay crying *mother mother*

as explosions echoed
off hills
of medicinal woods

i picked up my guitar

*

body a jeweled island
every hair a miracle
striped iridescent pearl

*

wishing for leaders who wear
lady slippers and look
after all sentient beings

guardian forest
deeming bear deer jay
horse dog and cat holy

trees reach for sun
gathering lifeforce

if drooping
they need rain

beech leaves wash my skin clean
when i press them to my face

*

dogwood giving perch
to nuthatch radiating gold

emptiness in form

*

let none of your air be injured
let none of your plants animals
or people experience suffering

spontaneous joy in my heart
hugging ancient pine

*

returning to my breath

ringing bells for peace

coyotes at dusk
sounding like wild women
laughing from caves
and rhododendron

growling and yipping
anthem of the forest

breath held listening to nina
singing *wild is the wind*

a deer in snow
danced fluidly towards cedar
wrapped in moss bark

my teacher saying stand up
against attacks on trans children
women people of color the holy
rhythms of our hands songs lips

i saw a pod of orcas
breach the turquoise water
they said *we're sick of screaming*
we need the sea to breathe

let food and medicine
homes and money be given
to everyone for free
rest for all

no more oil drilling
or enslaved mothers
on produce farms in factories

cages extinct
flowers and berries
planted by wild birds again
transporting and buying less
foraging and growing plants more
mountains left as they are
no new towers on holy hill
dogs running free

lead belly on the stereo
saying whoever's in the world
has a right to be

black eyed susans
supernovas comets moon gardens
body that opens to ocean

*

crabs walking with plastic tubs
instead of shells on their backs

on an island of plastic bottle caps
in the styrofoam pacific

*

whalebacks timber
skies and seas
recovering from being bombed
after nuclear testing

*

how do we behave responsibly

when the intelligence is never artificial
but always part of the living whole

skeleton keys

a painter banned from art during the regime
kept creating in secrecy
and buried each painting in the yard

the watercolors were of jellyfish that never die
they only get younger

giving root to feminine strength
and remedies for war

letting all vehicles be zero emission
and quiet produced without petroleum

returning to innocence
until the moment of rebirth

grandmothers from *no more deaths*

placed jugs of water at border crossings
for refugees in desert heat

officers from us border patrol dumped
the jugs of water on cacti

and arrested the grandmothers
for offering aid to humans in need

you lived in failed mill town
flooded with orange sludge
and dead fish from pollution

you went to the highlands for protection
turned to hendrix
for the wild
comfort of the milky way

mountain laurel petals
made umbrellas
to shelter you from acid rain

your teacher was don cherry's trumpet
your praise songs
purified the aquifers

you said *what are they doing*
pouring poison on mother sea

earth bounces back
when left alone
she doesn't need us

we're all one energy
you said *i can't wait*
till four years is over

may industry quiet down to hear
a whale's heartbeat our own breath

may orcas be able to meditate on a whale song
echoing from miles away

wanderer

burrowing in sand dunes
hidden by giant grasses

body translucent
river of my veins

connected to the sea halfway
underwater halfway in stars

washed by eternal waves
song of mystery

*

a woman knelt with liquor bottle
head bowed as if praying to the beach

cops shined flashlights on her
waves muting the powerplay

listening to you play heavy metal on guitar
you served tea
to your homeless friends
gave red and black paintings away

a gypsy wanderer said
we've all had trauma
we all deal with oppression

someone from north dakota
with anarchy skull tattoo
mumbled low smoking cigarettes
burning incense

you said *cool you hear the crows*
and played a tool song

lotus with pink hair
self-consciously rapped
life is music love

uncle told me
take an incubation
break   then make art
to produce the real thing

paying attention to dreams
is like nurturing a garden
the unconscious moves
so much faster than the conscious

choose purpose over prosperity

he painted the same basalt boulder
every day for a year in all weather
in sand dune blackberry shelter

his hardcopy of *pilgrim at tinker creek*
my introduction to dillard

birdlike i slept in tall pines
with white horse naying
ocean wind caressing me
making me strong

hammock cradling me
held by ponderosas
coyotes howling in the dark

hiking in red sand
i thought *i need to orient myself*

i looked up at the sun
time seemed to stop

i heard a creature rustling

a large black and gold lizard
emerged with its baby

the child lizard
rode on its mother's back

nodding to the sun
dragons carrying the light

leading to flower water
in a dry scorched place

spirals painted on pink stones

listening to stories
while making wreaths
in farmhouse garage

don said at the hilltop diner
easter morning
people smoked meth outside
a guy came in with painted-on
skintight pants
no shirt cowboy hat
went to the jukebox
and played *shout at the devil*
the bartender turned it up real loud
everyone rocked out
the nine customers didn't care

a woman in a muumuu
ran down the street yelling
in snow as she chased a man
took his metallica shirt
and put it on over her muumuu

the *ride the lightning* shirt
was then burned in the street

hearing *spanish caravan*
through bedside boombox every night
morrison's singing took me away
over balsam precipice

where i drank melted snow
used cedar boughs as blankets
wore a string of ash berries
carried twigs of hemlock

a large buck with antlers
stood upright facing me
surrounded by fawn
guiding a deer
wearing black robe
onto a saddled horse
hidden in forest

blue heron welcomes me
to the living waters
not like the drunks at home

cold fast river and red pine
say *here you go*
clean your eyes
you are my child
and always will be

reservoir

whitecaps come onto shore
seagulls hovering above me

the benefit of cold
gusts is my aloneness
no one here but me and spirit
my past and future
blooming through infinity
tent walls flapping wildly
a hysterical moment that will soon pass
tarp a flag saying *here i am*
grounded with earth
a child pretend camping

laughing at how the storm shakes the tent
i would like to fly

*

lakeside i dreamed
a voice said *nothing material can*
satisfy the hunger of the soul

feeling it's enough to be alive
with illuminated horses
in sunlit fields unreal golden
against shadowy asphalt
creatures rustling
through tunnels of wheat
relocating to the quiet
hidden peace

travel log

saturday night
moments sacred with you
by flooded river
ice crystals speaking

fir trees levitating
on frozen bog

wishing for animal helpers
and guardians in all living things
to surround you

friday
listening to *falling* on the bus
wearing headphones

sun flashing on elderly passengers

watching the damaged earth
dead hawk on the median
passing through tunnels

gate thirty-three going to los angeles

sunday
where they lie on the beach at christmas

mary said there's a whale under the pier
that keeps all her lost things

joe said it's always been nice with mary
twenty years of easy love

monday
i disappeared through
palmy red desert
flower murals along freeways
asking *where is the goddess here*

a black coyote ran through
gas station orange moon
factories on desert floor

a man on the bus said
soon there will be no place
for blackbirds and that ain't funny

tuesday
sound of pixies
and led zeppelin booming outdoors

red balloon rising
a transmission to you
atop golden butte

you texted me
hope you find tranquility
in the desert

subtle energies connecting us
across distances

wednesday
land of no clean tap water
throwing away millions
of water bottles each day

cooks at the casino with no green cards
mexicans being deported from mexico

*

walking into huge music store
playing the same melody on all
the classical guitars

thursday
i couldn't find my ticket
but the plane still took me

i took the keys
from everywhere i stayed
and found them
in my pockets later
glittering in strange places

*

hearing your songs
through headphones feeling both
like i've recently been
granted everything
and like i have only myself

*

you arrived at o'hare right after me
sparrows seeking
each other in winter rain

friday
all matter shifting
currents swirling

i hold onto the one
inside my chariot

on the riverbank
watching it all go by

my boat drifts

teeth chiseled logs
guarding beaver
den hidden
in sand burrows

at home in silt
black ripples
alive with
each movement

living off bark
ferns and cattail

making water
clear for fish

tiger swallowtail
flying over
shimmering current

ever present
teaching us
to glow
with jewelweed

swim in silent
tree prayer

thousands of thrushes
sparrows geese ducks swans
gliding overhead each night

auspicious voyagers
coming down to taste

the honey of everywhere
first time here

making plainsong
of wingbeats

in meteors we sleep
in down feather shelter

*

we never camped with tents
we laid in sleeping bags
directly on the earth

stars our tent
we never camped in campgrounds
we slept in parks we biked to

in grassy fields on roadsides
on shores of salt lakes   in arms
of canyons above the river

wild friend

the fool's heart
became a flame
humming praises
to the one
that sustains us

black gold earth servants
  hugging bergamot in rain

         when i spoke gently to bees
         they purred

      sleeping under silk blue petals
       trusting mother completely

telepathically in tune
  covered in squash blossoms

       you said being close to humming bees
       reduces stress

soothing me with homeopathic pollen
  bees smiling when i talk to them

bats cleanse the earth and air
keeping plants
from being eaten by beetles

bats forage over wetlands
fully alive and aware

      i said *hi i'm glad you're here*
      walking to creek shrine

the most sensitive listeners
can hear my every thought

sleeping upside down
wild joyful faces
ready to soar

      bats navigate by echolocation
      gliding through meteors
      chanting rosary prayers

the house bat knew
to fly out the door

calmed down
when i turned off
the electric fan

      let there be sheltering oaks
      and selenite caves
      balm on bat ecosystems

here is the juniper

moss-covered granite
here is the scarred birch starlit
throne   here are the hemlock
grandmothers   the trickling inlet
here is the bear's home
i'm only a guest in

spotted salamander

rain being glistening in flood
rising to higher ground

standing perfectly still
one with the path

mysterious witness
always listening

may all who are thirsty
drink clear water

blending with hazel and polypore
knower of labyrinths

tying purple ribbons
to conifer branches

to say *let all creatures be
respected and free*

scent of wet spruce returning melted snow
coming down from the mountain
finding remnants of a fallen crow
first i've ever seen
quiet grave by the stream
marked by a few feathers
and a grandmother's hand
descendent of oldest living being
life is always supported
by the bones of death
and humus of decay
climbing the footpath
on thawed trails of dead leaves
to glowing rock guardians
where snow still glistened
beech leaves rattling a song
calling all light
all is me
in another world
wrapped in holy gold
there the new day shine bathes us
summiting hilltop magically
then racing back down smiling

let us guard snakes
living in grassy holes
rock walls and milkweed patches

        ribbon snakes
        with yellow stripes
        garters carnelian ringnecks

purple milk snakes
humble in enlightened knowing
waiting to reveal themselves as guides

        symbol of our chakras
        in myth saying to bless not curse
        and be blessed not bitten

shedding skin
in secrecy
becoming new

i never knew squirrels went swimming
until i saw you

doggy paddling across the lake
in mirror waters reflecting clouds

you looked like a small duck
or muskrat tail afloat luminescent

you jumped onto silver
driftwood bridge and ran ashore

thank you wild god with me
staying hidden and indomitable

knowing how to heal yourself
in purest minerals on earth

brown toad facing east
hiding in tulsi
only its head visible

dreamy eyed
amidst purple flowers
the very light within

loons sang

the island swayed
red reflection
the pond sang
and changed
loons danced
and showed
white bellies
cedar fed
the sun

barbed wire surfacing
from wet soil near weasel tree

earth telling me
how they once barbed her

a crown of thorns
now softened by leaf

in the car taking note
of clearcut forests
paved for new freeway

bo diddley singing
you don't love me
you don't care

returning from depths
of pulsing star

beaver with velvet fur
circled me
in grassy reeds

      splashing diamonds
      with paddle tail

the carver water router
weaver   knower

resting in spatterdock
hidden from trappers

      i swam at silver stone
      waded through milk foam

opened my eyes in the swim
seeing golden rocks breathe

i gathered pine needles
to make a tea like beaver makes

      i had the thoughts of beaver
      and they had my thoughts
      let all beings have merciful protection
      like these waters give

mother orb carrying us home

hersch and spalding on the stereo
       riding through turkey fields

girl and boy jumping
       on trampoline holding hands

crows walking down the highway mandala art
       dogs on train tracks

low tide sandbar
       wearing hat and glasses as shield

empty dirt parking lot
       black feather trailhead crown

osprey catching a fish then releasing it
       to blue sheen

ice water submersion
       resetting me

climbing pink granite
       egg shaped boulders

boots floating
       with rock crabs

leaves of seaweed
       rising from the waterwheel

rowan garlands
       for the waxing moon

porcupine walking up to me
  from forest orbs

mother divine holding us
  as we orbit her

*

tall pine guru
  saying *meditate under me*

sunflowers sustain
  you from within

crow flying over
with sumac berry
my anti-depressant

paper birch covered
in mist the gift
the mountain holds

a small ringneck snake
found its way inside
i let it out before the storm

every object celestial
every stone a piece of star

blessed virgin in cherry wood
alder watching over me

*

serpents who feel earth's heartbeat
with their whole being

wishing harmlessness
towards everything

*

door covered in moths
body covered in north star

walking to shore after sleep
so foggy i couldn't see the lake
till i was right next to it
looked like i was paddling without hands
under trees not yet planted

kayaking a lake that doesn't exist
within clouds where bear swims
without anyone seeing
who walks with mouth open
speaks taste

bathed in chamomile
scent of hazelnuts blooming

*

land rights and jurisdiction
given back to tribes

*

stars of the big dipper turned bear
swimming the lake with me

pollen skin
the wild friend
i'm enveloped in

divine life support
giving breath
each second

*

crickets singing
in tempo to *buffalo gals*

take me
the birds sing with me

tent window
become mother's face
in the night

birch roots her lotus feet
my refuge

with frogs and snakes nearby
i slept safely with the earth
at the mercy of ma
like all beings
graciously sharing a home
with humyns

power of loon singing
we are all divine

haloed one
reverberating sound
throughout the whole
universe dancing
over water

milkweed feathers

thistle silk in my hands

owl invocations at dusk

*

the miracle of existing
of having a body

guarded by dragonflies

*

juncos jeweling the yard

on the news endangered

right whale named medusa
entangled in fishing gear

    star of the sea saying
    untie me

bats released in secrecy
by the river in ukraine
to keep them
from being bombed
at rehabilitation center

refugees crossing rapids
to escape the war

*

mary waving to a bus
of immigrant arrivals
welcoming them to nyc
sharing her house
food and bicycle

carrying upturned moss
like a fragile bird
and replanting it
on sapphire stone

eating spruce sap
in cinnamon fern

telling deer *stay in caves*
safe from predators

barred owl
with mother face
flying low
through trees
my blessing
from the mere
sight of a saint

keen listener
saying om at twilight
stargazer seer
in the dark knower
of wild tracks
on wet stones
all fluid cedar throb

i wrote poems on hemlock trunks
using my fingertip
dipped in creek water
the way the oracle said to

tiny bead-shaped cones
taught me
the art of letting go

mystic rose pink sun
walking on ocean sand
saying we're already in a bardo

able to attune
to light streaming
from our hands

bringing radiance

athlete youth in france
jumped on clock towers
using superhero moves
to turn off wasteful
electric night lights

*

luck of no streetlamps now

just glowing embers

coyotes looking otherworldly
running uphill mighty and agile
my parents when i'm feral

*

following hoof prints
emerging invisible
cleaned howling protector

cedar berries floating
fragrant medicinal

water knowing me
cradling me

body a robe of soul

in lily of the valley groves
amidst sensitive ferns

squirrels the eyes of the maple
cleansed by breath of bark

all filled with sun
even in the dark

*

isis birthing
the savior like mary

moonlit clouds
flying over lapis sky

*

a black dog beside her

mother treats all
her children with love

stirring the ocean
with healing hands
blessing all sharks
whales turtle
coral sealions
barnacles kelp forests
seahorses stones

golden guide
giving life
to all hearts
of the earth

*

now you rest
put your feet up
and have something
to eat mother

strawberries for mary

flowers moving as i move
earth and spirit
dancing as i dance
shimmering with life

ruby hummingbird
face of a little saint
drinking jewelweed

butterflies with citrine wings
fragile yet strong

wishing for all to have
divine forcefields
turtle shells around them
balsam after rain

ascending far beyond the names
others gave them

raven a star
balancing on
tallest spruce
helping spread pollen
bowing to auroras

tossing leaves
into the sun

holy glitter
making me
a child again

                                        carrying broken
                                        stones falling stars
                                        becoming ocean

salutations to you

sun who is the source of all
perfect light inside

i am alive
your illuminated brilliance
gives me all

cradled in blue ridges streams
leading to shining peaks
overlooking jeweled island

neon green mosses
hemlock elders
waiting to be heard

supreme friend
you must be honored
and protected

look at your veins
pulsing   the unbelievable
miracle of your skin
your perfect lips
bringing me only
the most needed words
of assurance

good air good light
good water
good lightning

the soothing words
you are the dawn

whispering tenderness
to each cell of my body
to each cell
of universe

you are powerful
you are whole
you know
everything

the sight of kindness heals me
my right hand
massaging my left hand

robins laughing

oh nucleus of life
i believe in you

pulsing star
who gives to all
let me not forget you

acknowledgments

thank you to the editors of the following publications: *honoring our ancestors anthology, maintenant, new feathers anthology*, and *rivers of ink anthology* for first publishing several of these poems in their earlier stages

and special thanks to aurelia and spuyten duyvil editors for all your support

notes

tributaries

rock me on the water by linda ronstadt

catch the wind by donovan

the healer inspired by a story in zora neale hurston's *mules and men*

litany

i'm inside all inspired by words of the goddess in *devi mahatmyam*

wild is the wind by nina simone

a nod to the bob dylan song *if dogs run free*

in the world by lead belly

wanderer

spanish caravan by the doors

falling by philip selway

wild friend

fool's heart inspired by the *rig veda* and nammā<u>l</u>vār

may all who are thirsty inspired by jesus in john 4:10

oldest living being refers to the crow bhuśunda in *vasistha's yoga*

the myth is *the serpent mother* from *folktales from india* edited by a.k. ramanujan

a loon gives satyakama spiritual teachings in the *chandogya upanishad*

while writing nature of infinity i was thinking about how language can be used to soothe and build up rather than negate and tear down life   the earth has always been my refuge and i was intentionally turning to the land for support   i wanted to express some of the majesty i see in nature and be grateful   these poems also intersperse recollections from my travels   feelings around the news and coping with loss   inner foraging   musical influences   and wishing affirmations of freedom and happiness for the many lifeforms

*

bees submerging themselves
in pitchers of celestial gold

pond spiraling infinity signs
a flower protecting the whole

www.ingramcontent.com/pod-product-compliance
Lightning Source LLC
Chambersburg PA
CBHW020743130626
46554CB00006B/2117